1000 Years of Scottish Churches
Early nineteenth century churches: 1800 to the Disruption of the Church of Scotland in 1843

John R. Hume

St Paul's Scottish Episcopal Church (St Paul's and St George's), Edinburgh

© John R. Hume, 2018
First published in the United Kingdom, 2018,
by Stenlake Publishing Ltd.
www.stenlake.co.uk
ISBN 978-1-84033-813-3

The publishers regret that they cannot supply
copies of any pictures featured in this book.

Printed by
Berforts, 17 Burgess Road, Hastings, TN35 4NR

Dedication

To everyone who has been responsible for the creation and maintenance of church buildings in Scotland over the last 1000 years

Acknowledgements

My prime acknowledgement is to my family, my wife Hope and my sons Matthew, Kenneth, Peter and Colin for their support over many years, and my father William Hume who introduced me to churches of a wide variety of denominations: without them this series of books could not have been written

Over a lifetime of involvement with church buildings I have cause to thank the many people who have given me insights both into individual congregations and into church organisation. I am particularly grateful to the Church of Scotland for periods of service as an Advisory Member of the General Trustees and as a member of the Committee on Artistic Matters (now the Committee on Church Art and Architecture). While I worked with what is now Historic Environment Scotland as an Inspector of Ancient Monuments, and subsequently as an Inspector of Historic Buildings I had opportunities to visit many of the buildings included here. I am also very grateful to the staff of Historic Environment Scotland, and particularly Veronica Fraser, for supplying me with digital copies of some of my photographs.

As a founder member of Scotland's Churches Scheme and as a Trustee both of that body and of its successor, the Scotland's Churches Trust, I have developed a knowledge of the church estate throughout Scotland which in a very direct way prepared the way for putting together this series. I am most grateful to my colleagues on both bodies.

It would be invidious to single out a few of the many individuals who have helped, but I feel that I must mention the late Frank Lawrie, my superior officer in Historic Scotland, who was very supportive of my work with churches. I would also like to thank Stenlake Publishing for undertaking the publication of this series, and the staff of the Mitchell Library, Glasgow for their assistance over the years.

Finally, I hope that my many friends in church and architectural circles will realise that they are all included in these expressions of gratitude.

Further Reading

There are many histories of individual churches in Scotland, variable in quality, but none negligible. Most of them concentrate, understandably, on congregational life, and often say very little about church buildings, but all are worth reading to build up a rounded history of the Church in Scotland. In the preparation of this series of volumes I have found the following more comprehensive books particularly useful:

Ewing, The Rev W, *Annals of the Free Church of Scotland*, T and T Clark, Edinburgh, 1914

Groome, FH (ed), *An Ordnance Gazetteer of Scotland*, 2nd edn, William Mackenzie, Edinburgh and London, c1895

Hay, G, *The Architecture of Scottish Post-Reformation Churches, 1560-1843*, Oxford University Press, 1957

Hume, JR, *Scotland's Best Churches*, Edinburgh University Press, 2005

Lamb, The Rev JA (ed) and Macdonald, *The Rev FAJ (ed), Fasti Ecclesiae Scotticanae: Ministers of the Church of Scotland, vols I-XI*, various publishers and dates

Lamb, The Rev JA (ed), *The Fasti of the United Free Church of Scotland, 1900-1929*, Oliver and Boyd, Edinburgh, 1956

Small, The Rev R, *Congregations of the United Presbyterian Church, 1733-1900*, David M Small, Edinburgh, 1904

Various authors and publishers, *The Buildings of Scotland* and The Royal Incorporation of Architects in Scotland *Architectural Guides* series.

Also the Sacred Scotland series of handbooks and other publications of the Scotland's Churches Scheme and the Scotland's Churches Trust.

Series Introduction

The oldest churches in Scotland for which we have firm above-ground evidence appear to date from the early-mid-11th century. Before that, however, there were probably wooden churches, as found in excavations at Whithorn. There are also the round towers at Brechin, Abernethy and Egilsay which may be earlier than the earliest surviving parts of stone churches. The establishment of focal points for Christian worship probably pre-dates the construction of church buildings, and many of the surviving free-standing sculptured crosses may have been intended for that purpose. Good examples of such crosses can be seen at Aberlemno, Glamis and Logierait in southern Pictland, and at Nigg, Shandwick and Hilton of Cadboll in northern Pictland. In what was Gaelic Scotland there are fine crosses at Kildalton, Islay and on Iona, while in the cradle of Christianity in Wigtownshire there are crosses in the Whithorn Museum and in the parish church of Kirkinner which probably fulfilled a similar role. This practice of marking 'sacred places' with stone monuments can probably be traced back from early Christianity into the Bronze Age and the Neolithic period.

The purpose of this series of volumes is not, however, to engage in debate, scholarly or otherwise, so it is fair to assume that the earliest roofed stone Christian churches are about a thousand years old. In the lecture I gave in 2014 for the Scotland's Churches Trust, I showed photographs of about 100 churches from the 11th to the 21st centuries, mostly existing buildings, but including some demolished during the past half-century or so. In preparing this series I have drawn on the material collected for that lecture, but have supplemented it by including many more churches which shed light, for one reason or another, on changes in church organisation, worship practice and architectural fashion over the millennium concerned. The original choice of buildings was explicitly personal: churches with a particular meaning for me by virtue of aesthetic appeal or association, or both. I have carried this through into the present collection, which also takes account of geographical and denominational diversity. This will, I hope, not be considered egotism: it is just that I believe that I cannot write honourably or convincingly in this context about buildings that do not have some real meaning for me. A handful, however, have been included because they 'ought' to be there; I will not identify them. A few years ago I wrote a book entitled *Scotland's Best Churches*, which concentrated on churches then in use. Here I have included churches not in use as such, roofless and ruined buildings, parts of buildings, and some now demolished. I have endeavoured to present a balanced selection of churches of different periods, denominations and architectural styles. In captioning I have concentrated on highlighting particular points of interest relating to the images, rather than giving 'potted histories' of the buildings concerned. The number of changes in the names of churches over the years has made it impossible to include them all; in a few instances I have included more than one. As far as possible the first name quoted is the original one. The assigning of dates is very difficult. I have chosen to list churches by date of completion rather than date of design or commencement of construction. I have used my judgement in interpreting the various dates to be found in published sources. Because old counties were an important context for church building I have used them in headings; modern local authority areas are not notably helpful.

Finally, please do not look on this collection as a work of scholarship (though I have done my best to make it scholarly). Look on it, rather, as a love-letter to the Church Universal. Each of these buildings is in its own way a place to encounter God, Father, Son and Holy Spirit, and to go out into the world imbued with the idea of loving God and loving our neighbours.

John R Hume
Glasgow
March 2018

SCOTLAND'S CHURCHES TRUST

Sustaining Scotland's places of worship.
15 North Bank Street, Edinburgh, EH1 2LP
0131 225 8644
Registered Charity: SC043105

From 1800 to the Disruption in 1843

There were so many churches built during the 19th century that I have divided that period into three. 1800 can be seen as an arbitrary date, but there is a real sense that the beginning of a new century can be seen as a watershed. In church design this was the period when the simple Gothic style, often referred to by architectural historians as 'Gothick' began to become fashionable. Landowners and town councils (heritors) had been responsible for church construction since the Reformation, and their increasing wealth and exposure to new aesthetic ideas affected the design of new churches. After the displacement of rural populations in the 18th century villages and small towns grew, and with them the demand for larger churches. In the second decade of the century a fashion developed for building larger buildings in what became known as 'Heritors' Gothic' style. Such churches were generally on compact rectangular plans, with towers either on one end, or on one side. These towers contained, or abutted staircases to give access to seating in galleries, which allowed large numbers of people to hear and see the ministers. Such churches were generally designed with features from English Gothic village churches, including pointed windows with tracery, buttresses and pinnacles. Often the towers contained clocks. Another variation on this embryonic Gothic was what has been termed the 'English College Chapel' style, especially suited to churches in streets, where only the frontage is visible. This was particularly favoured in this period by the Roman Catholic and Scottish Episcopal churches, both of which expanded markedly, partly as a result of migration from England and Ireland.

In church organisation a notable development was the coming together of most of the fragmented Secession congregations. This took place in 1820, when the United Associate Synod was formed, commonly known as the United Secession Church. The new denomination began to build new churches, generally in Classical style, for they associated the Gothic Revival with the Church of Scotland, Roman Catholic and Episcopal churches, whose beliefs they shunned. These churches, however, continued to build in Classical style throughout this period.

An important phenomenon during this period was the rapid growth of urbanisation and industrialisation. The old parish system, which was a civil as well as a religious one, came increasingly under strain, especially in Glasgow, where the administration of relief of the poor who were migrating from rural Scotland and Ireland was putting pressure on parishes. There was also an acute need for more and larger church buildings. At first the latter was addressed by constructing 'chapels of ease', buildings situated conveniently for new areas of housing, but with no civil responsibilities, and therefore no Kirk Sessions. The issue of Patronage also became more acute as the middle classes became more numerous and engaged to an increasing extent with church affairs. In the late 1830s the Patronage question became a high-profile concern, with a number of cases of 'intrusion' of ministers by heritors against the will of congregations.

At the General Assembly of the Church of Scotland in 1834 the issues of the provision of churches in areas of expanding population, and of Patronage were both addressed. The 'Chapels Act' was passed, authorizing the building of new churches and the carving out from existing parishes of 'Quoad Sacra' parishes, for purely religious purposes. The 'Veto Act' which allowed congregations to veto the appointment of ministers chosen by the Heritors (major landowners and burgh councils) was also passed. Because these measures adversely affected the heritors both Acts were challenged in the civil courts, which ruled in 1839 that the Veto Act, and early in 1843 that the Chapels Act, were contrary to civil law. By 1843 187 'quoad sacra' parishes had been created since 1834, all of whose ministers stood to lose their stipends and manses. It is not surprising, therefore that matters came to a head at the General Assembly in Edinburgh in May 1843, when a large proportion of ministers left the Assembly and, led by the Moderator, walked in procession to a hall in Canonmills where they constituted the Free Church of Scotland, leaving their churches, stipends (salaries) and congregations for an uncertain future.

Note: **D** after a caption means demolished: **A** means adapted to other uses or disused

St Clement's Parish Church, Dingwall, Ross and Cromarty

Constructed in 1799-1803, this is a late example of a large Classical burgh church, for the county town of Ross and Cromarty, and the furthest north of the type. The mixture if window shapes sits rather uneasily with the neat pediment and Classical steeple. The architect was George Burn of Haddington.

Skene Parish Church, Aberdeenshire

Skene was the first post-Reformation Gothic church in rural Aberdeenshire when it was built in 1801. The bellcote and the quatrefoil in the head of the gable were added in 1840 by Aberdeen architect John Smith, in 1840, emphasising the symmetry of the design.

Towie Parish Church, Aberdeenshire
This is a more typical early 19th century rural Aberdeenshire church, built in an upland area in 1803. The round-headed windows are typical of the period, contrasting with Skene's pointed windows.

Saltoun Parish Church, East Saltoun, East Lothian
This unique building, vaguely English in style, is in rural East Lothian, and dates from 1805. The designer was probably Robert Burn.

Comrie Old Parish Church, Perthshire

Comrie is a village on the edge of the Highlands. This church was constructed in 1803-05 and designed by John Stewart. It is notable for its combination of pointed 'Gothick' windows and Classical steeple. **A**

The Scottish Episcopal Church of St John the Evangelist, Pittenweem, Fife

From the late 18th century the Scottish Episcopal Church was increasingly tolerated by the civil authorities. This is an early 19th century small town example of an Episcopal church, with Gothic windows. It was constructed in 1805. The shallow chancel on the right was added in 1869-70.

Kildrummy Parish Church, Aberdeenshire
Situated in rolling countryside, this is a very fine example of a 'Gothick' parish church, built in 1805-06. This view shows the rear of the building; the entrance and the bellcote are on the front. The building is now in the care of the Scottish Redundant Churches Trust.

St Michael's Parish Church, Inveresk, Midlothian
Inveresk grew up as a very select residential area from the late 17th century, and this parish church (which also serves the town of Musselburgh) was appropriately both Classical and majestic. It was built in 1805 and designed by Robert Nisbet. Extensions at both ends, by J McIntyre Henry, made in 1893, can just be seen.

Bourtie Parish Church, Aberdeenshire

Bourtie is a rural parish between the towns of Inverurie and Oldmeldrum. It was built in 1807 by James Walker, mason and William Sangster, wright, on the site of an earlier church, and incorporates the bellcote (dated 1728) from that building. It is similar to, but smaller than, Kildrummy.

St Peter's Parish Church, Peterhead, Aberdeenshire

Peterhead is a town in the north-east of Aberdeenshire, and was remodelled in the late 18th and early 19th centuries by a consortium of Edinburgh men. They employed Alexander Laing, an Edinburgh architect, to design this building as a focal point in the settlement. In keeping with their rational concept of the development the church is Classical in style. It was completed between 1804 and 1806.

Echt Parish Church, Aberdeenshire

Echt is an estate village in a largely rural area. This is arguably the most attractive 'Gothick' church in north-east Scotland. It was built in 1804-06 for the 3rd Earl of Fife.

Logierait Parish Church, Perthshire

There is a broken Pictish cross-slab in the churchyard of Logierait, so this was an early Christian site. The present church was constructed in 1804-06 to designs by John Stewart to serve what must have been a large rural population. Internally, it was sub-divided in 1928 by J Jeffrey Waddell.

St Paul's Parish Church, Perth, Perthshire
This is a late example of an octagonal parish church, built in 1806-07 and designed by John Paterson. It was constructed to serve the growing city of Perth. Though somewhat ungainly, it is an early example of a large 'Gothick' church, and most unusually for that period for has a steeple.

A

St George's Tron Parish Church, Glasgow

As Glasgow developed to the west of the mediaeval core from the late 18th century new churches were needed. This one was built in 1807, situated axially in West George Street, looking towards George Square. It is still a notable feature of the city centre. The architect was William Stark, who died tragically young.

Bolton Parish Church, East Lothian

This little village church was built in 1809, and probably designed by Archibald Elliot. With its mixture of pointed and round-headed arched openings it is on the cusp of a radical change in parish church design. The entrance through the base of a tower at the front of the body of the church was to be developed in the next few years into what became known as 'Heritors' Gothic'.

Lochwinnoch Parish Church, Renfrewshire

The village of Lochwinnoch was enlarged from the 1780s as a cotton-spinning and hand-loom weaving centre, on a geometric plan. On the west side of a central square this octagonal Classical church was built in 1806-08 to replace a church in the older part of the village.

Culter Parish Church, Lanarkshire

Culter is a very attractive small village in upland south Lanarkshire. Its parish church was built in 1810, but later altered more than once. The tower and bellcote are unique in Scotland. **A**

Galston Parish Church, Ayrshire

This is a late example of a large burgh church with a Classical steeple, built in 1807-10 and designed by John Brash, presumably on the site of an earlier church. It sits on a mound in the centre of Galston, which was at that time a hand-loom weaving community.

Slamannan Parish Church, Stirlingshire
The village of Slamannan is on a very exposed upland site, and this church, built in 1810-11 by James Warden, wright in Falkirk, is suitably austere in appearance, reflecting not only its geographical situation, but also the form of worship conducted in it.

Fetteresso Parish Church, Stonehaven, Kincardineshire
This church is, unusually, on a D-plan. The military appearance was a fashion of the time. The building was constructed in 1810 to a design by John Paterson to replace a church on the outskirts of Stonehaven. It was enlarged in 1878 by James Garvie and Sons, builders in Aberdeen.

15

Falkirk Old Parish Church (Falkirk Trinity Parish Church), Stirlingshire

The mound in the centre of Falkirk on which this church is set may well have been an early place of worship. The oldest part of the existing church is the tower, which was built in 1734 and designed by William Adam. Most of the rest of the cruciform church was rebuilt in 1810, with some minor later additions.

Lesmahagow Old Parish Church, Lanarkshire

There was a mediaeval priory here, whose church probably remained in use as a parish church until 1810 when the body of this building was constructed. By that time the tower and Classical steeple seen in this view had already been built, in 1803. The church was extended to the east in 1894 to accommodate an organ. The excavated remains of some of the priory can be seen to the south of this building.

Dumbarton Old Parish Church (Riverside), Dunbartonshire

This elegant Classical burgh church was built in 1810-11 for the shipbuilding town of Dumbarton. It was designed by John Brash, architect of Galston Parish Church. This view shows the church dominated by the Dumbarton Distillery, opened in 1938 on the site of one of the town's shipyards.

Glenorchy Parish Church (Glenorchy and Inishael), Dalmally, Argyll

This church is a blend of the old and the new, with an octagonal body and otherwise in 'Gothick' style. It is on an island in the River Orchy. It was built in 1810-11 to designs by James Elliot. The metal window tracery dates from a renovation of the church in 1898 by Kenneth Macrae of Oban.

Old Kilpatrick Parish Church (Bowling and Old Kilpatrick), Dunbartonshire

The village of Old Kilpatrick lies on the north bank of the Clyde Estuary, and may have been the birthplace of St Patrick, patron saint of Ireland. This church was built on the site of an earlier building in 1812, in 'later English style', (otherwise 'Heritors' Gothic'). It was one of the first churches built in this manner, and became a model for others in the ensuing years.

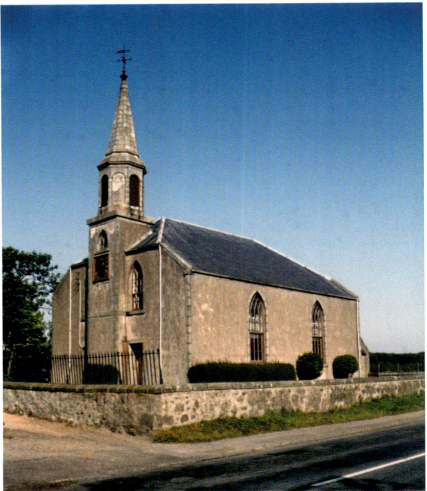

Crimond Parish Church, Aberdeenshire

Built to serve a rural Aberdeenshire village, Crimond blends a modest Classical steeple with pointed windows. It was built in 1811-12, possibly to designs by Robert Mitchell. The parish gave its name to a popular Scottish psalm tune.

The steeple of Libberton and Quothquhan Parish Church, Lanarkshire

This church is in the hamlet of Libberton, in upland Lanarkshire. The steeple can best be described as 'sub-Classical'. The plain building was constructed in 1812, and was restored in 1902.

Original Secession Church (The Apostolic Church), Edinburgh

Situated in Edinburgh's South Side, this is a good example of an early 19th century urban Secession church, very plain, but with a severely Classical entrance. It was constructed in 1813.

Mearns Parish Church, Renfrewshire

This church has already been included for its steeple of about 1755. This view shows the body of the church as substantially enlarged in 1813. The porch on the right was added in the 1920s; there is a matching one at the other end. The roof ventilator also dates from the 1920s.

Collace Parish Church, Perthshire

Built in 1813 in rural Perthshire on the site of a 12th century church (fragments of which survive in the churchyard), Collace is another early 'Heritors' Gothic' church, and more convincingly Gothic than Old Kilpatrick.

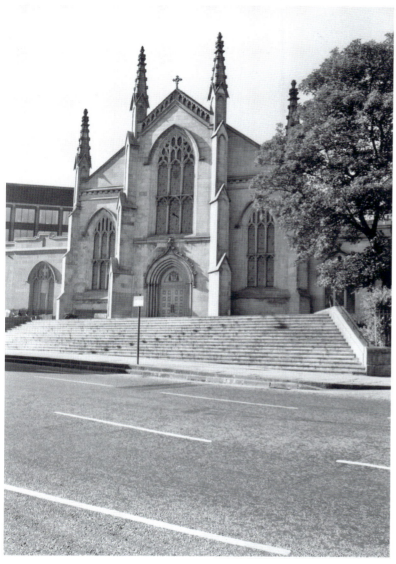

Kilmaronock Parish Church, Dunbartonshire

Set in countryside close to the south-eastern shores of Loch Lomond, this little church with its enormous round-headed windows is arguably the finest late-Georgian church in Scotland. The little domed-topped belfry does nothing to take away from the tremendous impact of these superb windows. The building was constructed in 1813.

St Mary's Roman Catholic Cathedral, Edinburgh

This was the first Roman Catholic church to be built in Edinburgh after the Reformation. The building was designed by James Gillespie Graham, and it was constructed in 1814. The façade is in what has been described as 'English College Chapel' style. Behind this frontage the church has been entirely rebuilt. Originally a chapel, it was designated a Cathedral in 1885.

Muirkirk Parish Church, Ayrshire
Muirkirk is an isolated community on the eastern edge of Ayrshire which came into being to serve an iron-smelting works in 1789. This squat and powerful building was built between 1812 and 1814 to designs by William Stark, who died before it was completed; it was finished by Thomas Smith. It was restored after a fire, in 1952-54, by Harry S McNair.

St George's Parish Church, Edinburgh
This monumental Classical church was designed by Robert Reid and built between 1811 and 1814 as the centrepiece of Charlotte Square at the west end of Edinburgh's New Town, on the axis of George Street, the New Town's central thoroughfare. The copper-clad dome is particularly striking. **A**

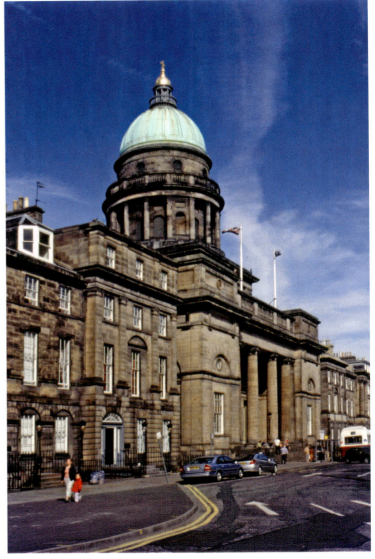

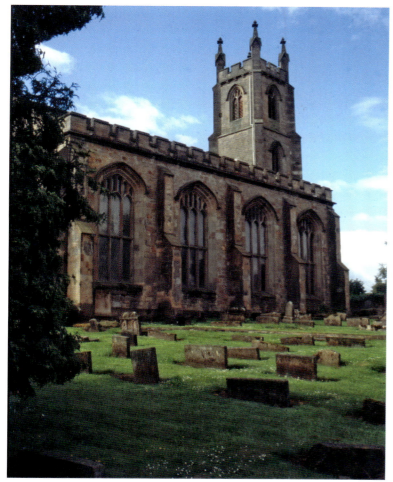

Clackmannan Parish Church, Clackmannanshire
This is a large 'Heritor's Gothic' burgh church, replacing an earlier church on this site, built in 1813-15, and designed by James Gillespie Graham, who was rapidly becoming the master of the early Gothic Revival in Scotland.

The steeple of Forfar Old Parish Church (Forfar East and Old), Angus
The body of this large burgh church dates from 1788-91, and was designed by Samuel Bell architect of St Andrew's Dundee. The building is hemmed in by street-frontage buildings, and a Classical steeple was added in 1814, also designed by Bell, probably to increase the visibility of the church. The steeple, resembling that of St Andrew's Dundee, dominates the town centre.

Nicolson Square Methodist Church, Edinburgh

Methodism was essentially an English non-conformist denomination, and early Methodist churches in Scotland were generally built to serve migrants from south of the Border. This is the finest early-19th century Methodist church in Scotland, and is deliberately not Gothic. It was designed by Thomas Brown and built in 1815-16.

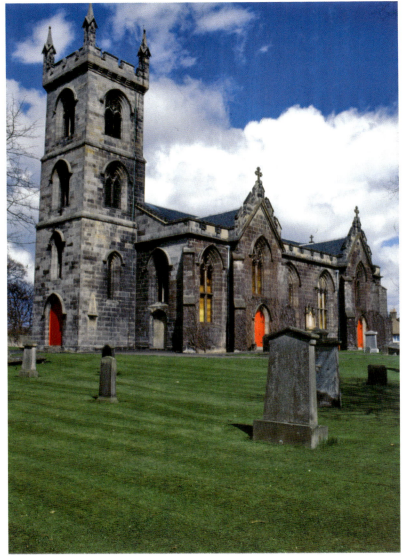

Liberton Parish Church, Edinburgh

Another Gillespie Graham building, this large Gothic Revival church was constructed in 1815 to replace an earlier building destroyed by fire. It was built to serve a parish on the southern outskirts of Edinburgh, and though its design has much in common with 'Heritors' Gothic' the layout is markedly different.

Erskine Parish Church (Bishopton), Bishopton, Renfrewshire
This building was designed by David Hamilton, a leading Glasgow architect, for a rural parish. It is another version of the 'Heritors' Gothic' concept, and was explicitly intended as a model for other churches. It was built between 1813 and 1815.

Albany Street Baptist Chapel, Edinburgh
Baptist churches in Scotland were in the early 19th century generally English in origin, and plain, simple buildings. This elaborate one, on the edge of Edinburgh's New Town, dates from 1816, and is very explicitly not a Gothic building. **A**

Kincardine-in-Menteith Parish Church, Perthshire
Designed by Richard Crichton for a rural parish, and constructed in 1814-16, this is
another interpretation of the 'Heritors Gothic' formula, and a very pleasing one.

Kilmorich Parish Church, Cairndow, Argyll
Situated at the head of Loch Fyne, Kilmorich was built in 1816 by Andrew
McKindley to replace a church of about 1700. As at Glenorchy the body of the
church is octagonal, but the design as a whole is very much simpler.

The steeple of Leith North Parish Church, Edinburgh

Leith is the port of Edinburgh, and was notably prosperous in the early 19th century. This church was built in 1813-16 to designs by William Burn, a leading Edinburgh architect of the period. It replaced an early post-Reformation church on another site. The building has a Classical portico, and is surmounted by this very elegant Classical tower and spire.

St Andrew's Roman Catholic Metropolitan Cathedral, Glasgow
This was the first Roman Catholic church built in Glasgow after the Reformation, and is sited very publicly on Clyde Street, on the edge of the city centre. Its elaborate design is by James Gillespie Graham, and it was built between 1814 and 1817 to serve the city's growing Roman Catholic population. Originally a chapel, it was designated a Cathedral in 1889.

St Andrew's Scottish Episcopal Cathedral, Aberdeen
Another, and very elegant, variation on the 'English College Chapel' formula, this church was built on the city's King Street as a statement of the revived status of the Scottish Episcopal Church. It was constructed as a chapel in 1816-17, and designed by Archibald Simpson, an Aberdeen architect. The porch was added in 1911 by Sir Robert Lorimer. Behind this façade the church has been largely rebuilt. It became a Cathedral in 1914.

St John's Scottish Episcopal Church, Edinburgh

Like St Andrew's, Aberdeen, this is a confident expression of the re-awakening of Episcopalianism, on a very public site at the west end of the New Town, in Princes Street. It was designed by William Burn in a very English Gothic style, and completed in 1815-18. The church was extended to the east in 1879-80 by Peddie and Kinnear.

Cockpen Parish Church, Midlothian

This imposing rural church was built in 1818 to replace an earlier church on a different site, which survives as a roofless ruin. The new church was designed by Archibald Elliot, incorporating details from the 'Heritor's Gothic' architectural language, but not unquestioningly. It is on a T-plan, with a strong emphasis on the central tower.

St Paul's Scottish Episcopal Church (St Paul's and St George's), Edinburgh

This church was built to designs by Archibald between 1816 and 1818, replacing a small 18th century church nearby. It is at the east end of the New Town. It was extended at the east end in the same style by Kinnear and Peddie. The Perpendicular Gothic treatment has echoes of that at Trinity College Chapel in Cambridge.

St George's Parish Church, Paisley, Renfrewshire

St George's was constructed in 1819 at a time when the town of Paisley was prospering as a centre of hand-loom weaving of fine textiles. The church was built to accommodate people who could not be housed in the Abbey Church. Paisley was a very design-conscious place, hence the generous, stylish 'flat-Palladian' treatment. It was intended to have a Classical steeple. **A**

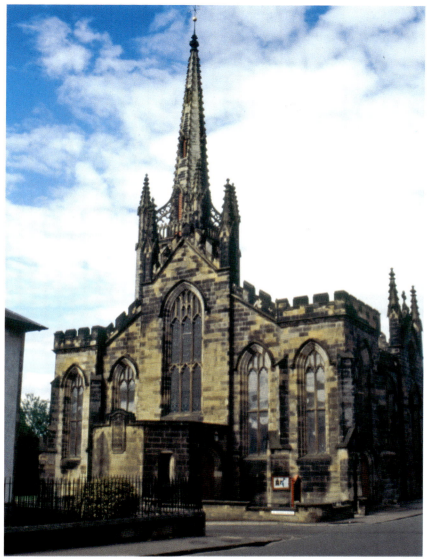

Logie Easter Parish Church, Ross and Cromarty
Another Gillespie Graham design, this church was built in 1818-19 for a rural parish in Easter Ross. The design is essentially that of a simplified 'Heritors' Gothic' building. The flattened tower is simple and effective. **D**

St Mungo's Parish Church, Alloa, Clackmannanshire
Designed by James Gillespie Graham for a wealthy burgh, this is an exuberant exercise in early English Gothic Revival, constructed in 1816-19. The steeple is based on that of Louth Parish Church in Lincolnshire. The porch in this view was added by Leslie Grahame Thomson in 1966-67.

Larbert Old Parish Church, Stirlingshire

Built in 1818-20 and designed by David Hamilton of Glasgow, this is a large, sophisticated and confident 'Heritor's Gothic' church. It is on a commanding site looking over the central Scotland rift valley.

Kirk o'Shotts, Lanarkshire

Situated high on moorland this large rectangular-plan Gothic Revival church used to be a conspicuous feature next to the M8 Glasgow-Edinburgh motorway until recent tree-planting. It was designed by James Gillespie Graham and built between 1819 and 1821. The large English Perpendicular windows are curiously at odds with the very modest bellcote.

The Rev James Hall's United Associate Synod Chapel (Broughton Place Parish Church), Edinburgh

In 1820 most of the congregations of the Secession churches (Burgher and Antiburgher) came together as the United Associate Synod and one of the first churches built by this body was this one, a fine exercise in the Greek Revival style for the New Town of Edinburgh dating from 1820-21. **A**

The steeple of Tarbolton Parish Church, Ayrshire

There was a late flowering of Classical steeples in Ayrshire. This is that of the village church of Tarbolton, and was designed by Robert Johnstone of Kilmarnock and built in 1819-21. The detailing is unusual but effective.

Duntocher United Associate Church (Duntocher West United Free Church), Dunbartonshire

The Rev James Hall's Edinburgh church was definitely a city-centre expression of Secession. This one, built in 1822 for a cotton-spinning community, is more typical of the deliberately plain but well-proportioned buildings favoured by Seceders.

Crossmichael Parish Church, Kirkcudbrightshire

This Galloway village church dates originally from 1751, and the tower appears to be original. The body of the church was enlarged in 1822, giving the appearance seen here, with tall pointed windows. The church is on a mound at the north end of its village, and is a notable landmark.

Hope Park Chapel of Ease, Newington, Edinburgh
As Edinburgh expanded in the early 19th century new churches were built to serve new suburban communities. This one is on the South Side, and was built in 1823 to a design by Robert Brown. The body of the church is in 'flat-Classical' style, and it is crowned by this tall and elegant cupola, rather than the steeple which one might have expected. **A**

St Mark's Scottish Episcopal Church, Portobello, Edinburgh

Portobello developed in the early 19th century as a fashionable seaside resort, as well as a smart residential suburb of Edinburgh. This unusual treatment of classical themes, dating from 1824, was presumably designed to appeal to a discerning congregation. The glazing of the windows is later, designed by Hay and Henderson.

Ettrick Parish Church, Selkirkshire

Situated in a remote part of the Southern Uplands this church was originally built in the 13th century. It was rebuilt in 1619, and again in 1824. The twin stairs to the gallery are remarkable.

St Mary's Parish Church (Broughton St Mary's Parish Church), Edinburgh

At the eastern edge of the New Town, this church was constructed by the City in 1824 to designs by Thomas Brown. The scale of the Classical body of the church is admirably set off by the tower and cupola. The church, in Bellevue Crescent, is the focal point of a new street to the east, Claremont Street.

Reformed Presbyterian Church, Stranraer, Wigtownshire

Not a Secession church, the Reformed Presbyterians trace their origin to the Covenanters who rejected the Episcopal church government imposed by Charles II, and also the State-sponsored Presbyterianism of 1689. Covenanting was strongest in south-west Scotland, and this little church in Stranraer, built in 1824-25, is the oldest surviving in the denomination.

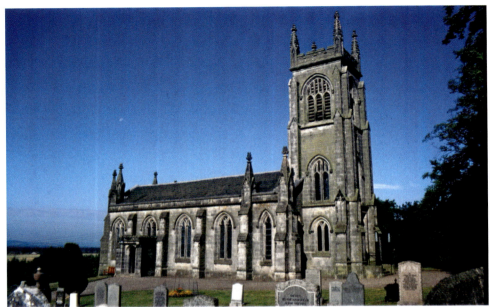

Lecropt Parish Church, Stirlingshire
This notably elegant 'Heritors' Gothic' church is on a hillside near Bridge of Allan, looking over the Carse of Stirling. It was designed by William Stirling I, and built in 1824-26 to replace an earlier church on this site. Its design has similarities to that of Larbert Parish Church.

Rafford Parish Church, Moray
Rafford is a rural parish in upland Moray, perhaps an unusual place to find this 'Heritors' Gothic' church by James Gillespie Graham, built in 1824-26. The tower pinnacles are heavier than one would expect from that architect.

Daviot Parish Church, Inverness-shire

This rural parish church is on a dramatic site overlooking the valley of the River Nairn (and the modern A9 trunk road). The building, with its slender steeple is a very distinctive landmark. It was built in 1826 by Thomas Macfarlane, mason and Donald Macphail, wright, to a specification by Alexander Grant.

Limekilns United Associate Church (Limekilns Parish Church), Fife

Limekilns was in the 1820s a little port of the Forth Estuary when this elegant Classical church was built by an United Associate congregation. That denomination favoured the Classical style, rejecting the Gothic Revival favoured by many heritors of the Church of Scotland at the time.

Dunino Parish Church, Fife

Dunino is a rural parish in eastern Fife, with this very refined English-Gothic parish church. It was designed by James Gillespie Graham and built in 1826. The porch on the right was constructed in 1928 to designs by J Jeffrey Waddell, who also added the chancel, on the left in this view.

Keiss Parish Church, Caithness

In the later 1820s the British Government, on the recommendation of Thomas Telford, gave grants to carve new parishes out of existing ones in the Highlands and Islands, and to build churches and manses to serve them. These buildings, to a range of standard designs, were the work of William Thomson, under Telford's supervision. This one, at the little fishing port of Keiss is an early example, dating from 1827, though slightly altered.

Rosemarkie Parish Church, Ross and Cromarty

Rosemarkie is a village on the south side of the Black Isle, overlooking the Cromarty Firth. This unusually elegant 'Heritors' Gothic' parish church was built in 1827 by Charles Falconer and John Wilson, masons, and James McLean, wright. The glazing of the windows was inserted in 1894 by John Robertson.

Kinlochbervie Parish Church (Kinlochbervie Free Church), Sutherland

This is another of William Thomson's Parliamentary churches. It was built in 1828 for a new parish in a remote area on the west coast of Sutherland. As seen here in 1976 it was in original condition, with cast-iron window frames made in Shropshire.

The Tron Parish Church, Edinburgh

Another church with a complex building history, it is included here because what we see here is partly of the 1820s. The building was first constructed to a design by John Mylne Junior between 1636 and 1647 for a congregation displaced by Charles I from the High Kirk of St Giles when he made it an Episcopal cathedral. The body of the building was cut back in 1785-87 by John Baxter Junior to the form seen here, and the steeple, destroyed in a fire in 1824, was rebuilt to a new design, by R and R Dickson in 1828.

A

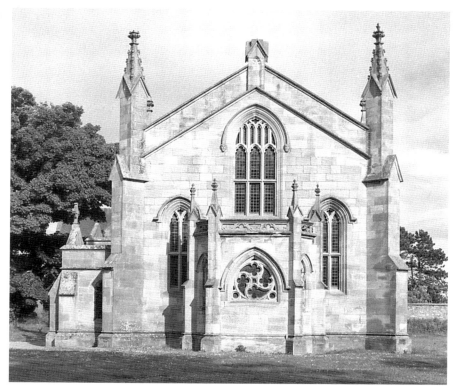

St Andrew's Scottish Episcopal Church, Fortrose, Ross and Cromarty
This is another church which is evidence of the revival of the Scottish Episcopal Church in the middle decades of the 19th century. A pleasingly simple Gothic church, it dates from 1828, and is in the manner of James Gillespie Graham.

St Mary's Roman Catholic Church, Fochabers, Moray
The revival of Roman Catholicism in north-east Scotland from the 1820s parallels that of the Scottish Episcopal Church. This small but refined 'College Chapel' building by James Gillespie Graham was built in 1828 and is evidence of that phenomenon.

St Stephen's Parish Church, Edinburgh

Like St Mary's, Broughton this church was built by the Town Council of Edinburgh to cater for the extension of the New Town. Axially situated at the foot of St Vincent Street, it is on a vast scale. It was designed by William H Playfair and built in 1827-28. Its square plan is set on a diagonal to the monumental tower. **A**

Cortachy Parish Church, Angus

Utterly different in scale, aesthetic and intent from St Stephen's, Cortachy was built in 1818-29 as an estate church for Cortachy Castle. It is in English Perpendicular style, and was designed by David Paterson. The projection on the end in this view is the Airlie Mausoleum, built for the landowners, the Earls of Airlie.

Stenton Parish Church, East Lothian

This is an East Lothian village church, built for the local landowner in 1829 to replace an earlier church, and designed by William Burn. Though from this view it looks like a typical 'Heritors' Gothic' building it is in fact a T-plan building, with a wing to the rear.

St John's Parish Church, Montrose, Angus

Constructed in 1827-29 for an overflow congregation from Montrose Parish Church, the Classical St John's was built at a time when Montrose was a prosperous textile town and seaport. The short cupola is an unusual feature.　**A**

Wick Old Parish Church (Wick St Fergus Parish Church), Caithness

This is a large burgh church constructed between 1820 and 1830 to replace an earlier building on the same site when Wick was flourishing as a centre for the herring-fishing industry. The sturdy, rather plain appearance of the church seems appropriate for the often stormy weather in this wild county.

Dalgety Parish Church, Fife

When built in 1830 in English Perpendicular style, this was a country church in West Fife. It was designed by William Burn to replace a mediaeval church (St Bridget's) whose roofless remains survive beside the Forth, in State care.

Cawdor Parish Church, Nairnshire

This church was built in 1829-30 by John Wilson. mason and John McIntosh, wright, to replace an early 17th century building. The porch of that church, seen in this view, was incorporated in the new building, which seems to have been deliberately antique in its style.

Monzie Parish Church, Perthshire

Another church by William Stirling I, this is significantly different from his church at Lecropt. Monzie is a rural parish near Crieff, on the edge of the Perthshire Highlands. This church is pleasingly simple; the porch is an addition to the church which was built in 1830-31 to a design by William Stirling I.

The tower of Aberdeen North Parish Church

Aberdeen North is another example of a church built to cater for the expansion of a city in the 1820s. It was built between 1829 and 1831 to designs by John Smith, a local architect of distinction. This refined Classical tower exemplifies not only the skill of the architect but also the rational expectations of the city at that time.   **A**

Aberdeen South Parish Church

This is another Aberdeen city centre church built at the same time as Aberdeen North (1830-31) by the same architect. Its elegant square pinnacled tower sits in front of a T-plan church, comparable with Cockpen Parish Church. In the right background is the spire of St Nicholas Parish Church, the 'Mither Kirk' (mother church) of the city, and more specifically of the North and South churches.   **A**

The Gordon Chapel (Scottish Episcopal), Fochabers, Moray

In a short street leading off the central square of the Ducal village of Fochabers, the Gordon Chapel was built in 1832-34 to designs by Archibald Simpson. Constructed at the expense of Elizabeth, wife of the 5th Duke of Gordon, it was designed with the worship-space on the first floor, with a school below. In 1874, when a new village school had been built, the lower level was converted into a rectory.

Dalry Parish Church, St John's Town of Dalry, Kirkcudbrightshire

The present church here was built between 1830 and 1832 to a design by William McCandlish, replacing a mediaeval church, of which the Gordon Aisle survives as a roofless ruin. The 1830s church is a variant of the 'Heritors' Gothic' model, with the tower in the centre of a long wall of a rectangular building.

The Parish Church of St Peter, Thurso (The Parish Church of St Peter and St Andrew), Caithness

A very confident and imposing example of a 'Heritors' Gothic' building, this church was constructed as a centrepiece in the 'new town' of Thurso in 1830-32. It was designed by William Burn, of Edinburgh, and is one of the best of his churches. It replaced the old, partly mediaeval church of St Peter.

Duirinish Parish Church, Isle of Skye, Inverness-shire

This is a very neat little 'Gothick' church near Dunvegan on Skye. It was built in 1832 to replace a late-17th century church on another site, which survives as a roofless ruin. The design of the tower of this church resembles that of Logie Easter Parish Church in Easter Ross.

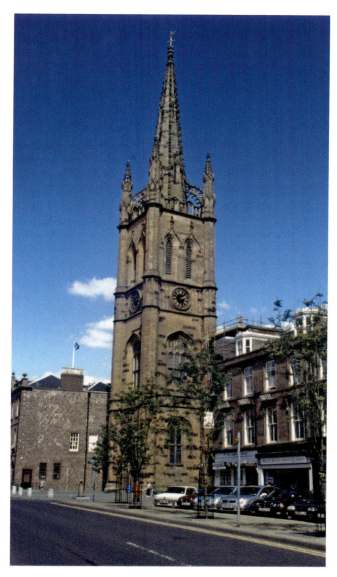

Montrose Old Parish Church, Angus

The body of this building was constructed in 1791 as a large burgh church, but the west front and remarkably tall tower and steeple were added in 1832-34 to a design by James Gillespie Graham. The steeple, like that of St Mungo's, Alloa, is modelled on that of the parish church of Louth in Lincolnshire. The height of the spire was probably intended to act as a seamark for the harbour of the town.

Tulliallan Parish Church (Tulliallan and Kincardine Parish Church), Kincardine-on-Forth, Fife

Built in 1833 to replace a 17th century building, this is another variant on the 'Heritors' Gothic' theme. There is a twin-gabled wing to the rear of the transverse range behind the tower. The earlier church, with a fine tower, still survives, though roofless.

St Margaret's Roman Catholic Church, Huntly, Aberdeenshire
The unique design of this church, with an octagonal worship space and baroque entrance front and tower, is further evidence of the growing confidence of the Roman Catholic revival in north-east Scotland. It was built in 1833-34, and was designed by William Robertson and the Rt Rev James Kyle. The expense of its construction was largely met by the Gordons of Wardhouse, sherry merchants.

Wallacetown Parish Church, Newton-on-Ayr, Ayrshire
This church was built in 1834 to serve the growing settlement of Newton-on-Ayr, a suburb of Ayr on the north side of the River Ayr. Its rather military style is unusual. The architect was John Kay, and the wings were added in 1903 by JK Hunter.

St Mark's Unitarian Chapel, Edinburgh
The Unitarian Church is a distinctive but small denomination more popular in England than in Scotland. This is the Edinburgh chapel of the Unitarians, and was built in 1834-35 to designs by David Bryce in a remarkably florid baroque style, to mark it out as a church in an otherwise residential terrace.

St Leonard's Chapel of Ease (St Leonard's Parish Church), Perth

In the 1830s there was a vogue for building 'chapels of ease' for the Church of Scotland in new housing areas, for the convenience of residents. This one, on the south-western edge of Perth, was designed by WM MacKenzie in a mixture of Greek and Italian styles, giving a monumental dignity to a fairly small building. between 1820 and 1830.   **A**

Monigaff Parish Church, Minnigaff, Kirkcudbrightshire

Minnigaff is a suburb of Newton Stewart, on the east bank of the River Cree. This church was designed by William Burn in a style similar to his village church at Stenton, East Lothian. Built in 1834-36, it replaced an earlier church whose roofless ruin survives in the graveyard.

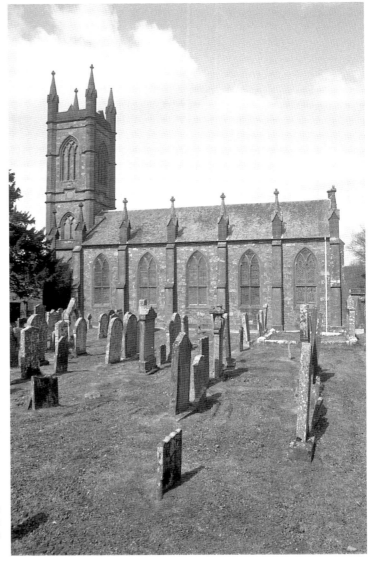

Ardchattan Parish Church, Achnaba, Argyll

This church is a conspicuous feature on the north side of Loch Etive. It was built in 1836 and designed by John Thom of Oban. Fairly plain externally, it has a very fine interior, with a long Communion table and an elegant Georgian pulpit.

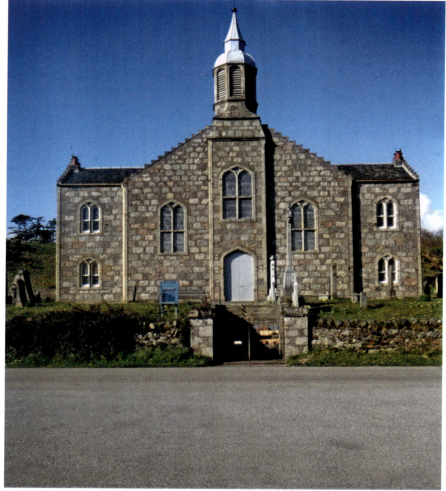

St Andrew's Roman Catholic Chapel, Dundee

St Andrew's was designed by George Mathewson and built in 1835-36, appropriately in 'English College Chapel' style, as used in several other early-19th century Scottish Roman Catholic churches The building was designated a Cathedral in 1923.

Sandwick Parish Church, Orkney

Originally constructed in 1835-36, this country parish church is on the west side of the Mainland of Orkney. It is the epitome of the small rural parish church. This view shows it as restored by the Scottish Redundant Churches Trust, in whose care it now is.

The Glasite Meeting House, Edinburgh

The Glasites have already been mentioned in connection with their octagonal Dundee church. This is their Edinburgh building, constructed in 1835-36, and the last church of the denomination. It is now in the care of a Trust. **A**

Forfar Congregational Church, Angus

Congregationalism was introduced into Scotland in the mid-17th century, but declined thereafter, until a late-18th century revival. It was, and remains, a modest denomination, and this Forfar church, built in 1836, is suitably plain.

Hope Street Relief Church, Lanark

The Relief Church seceded from the Church of Scotland in 1761, and became popular in town and cities. Its churches tended, like this one, to be domestic in scale, and mildly Classical, like this one in Lanark, built in 1836-37. **A**

St Mary's Roman Catholic Church, Inverness

Built in 1836-37 as the Roman Catholic chapel for Inverness this building was designed by William Robertson, architect of St Margaret's, Huntly, but in a very different style. This one is in a rich 'College Chapel' style, and is a conspicuous feature of the north bank of the River Ness in the centre of Inverness. It has been largely rebuilt internally.

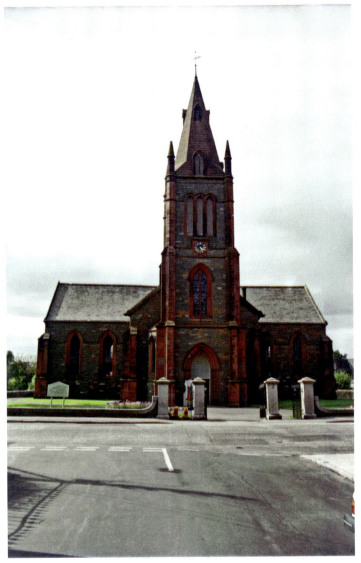

Kirkcudbright Parish Church, Kirkcudbrightshire

Towards the end of the 1830s Gothic Revival churches in Scotland began to be constructed with steeples. Apart from the precocious St Paul's, Perth this one, built in 1835-36, may be the first. It is in the centre of the picturesque town of Kirkcudbright, and was designed by William Burn as a large burgh church.

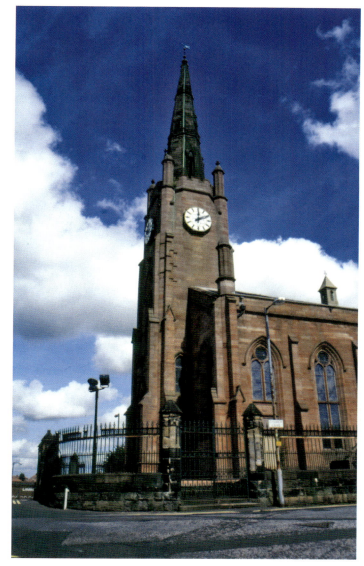

Airdrie Reformed Presbyterian Church, Lanarkshire
The Reformed Presbyterians have already been mentioned in the context of their Stranraer church. This is the Airdrie one, built in 1838. It is notably severe, reflecting the rigour of the tenets of this denomination.

The steeple of Gartsherrie Chapel of Ease (New St Andrew's Parish Church), Coatbridge.
Built in 1839, this steepled Gothic Revival church was designed by Scott, Stephen and Gale as the centrepiece of a part of Coatbridge developed by William Baird and Co, ironmasters, in connection with their nearby Gartsherrie Ironworks. The church is on a hilltop, emphasising the height of this steeple.

Alyth Parish Church, Angus

This is another early steepled church but not Gothic. Instead it is in a style variously described as 'Saxon', 'British' or just 'Romanesque'. It was designed by Thomas Hamilton and built in 1836-39 as the burgh church for a textile town.

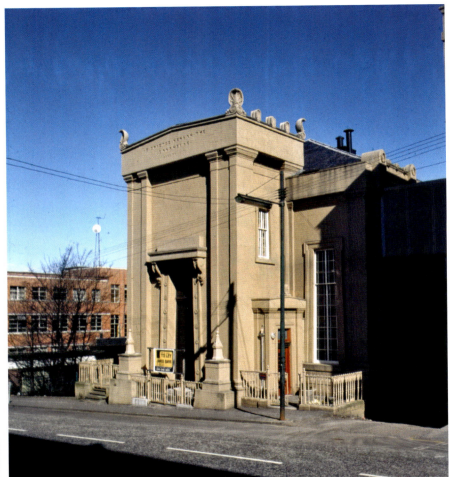

St Jude's Scottish Episcopal Church, Glasgow

To serve the fashionable Blythswood Estate development to the west of Glasgow city centre, St Jude's was built in 1838-39, to an Egyptian-inspired design by John Stephen, for a Scottish Episcopal congregation. There was originally a cupola above the central doorway.

A

St Margaret's Roman Catholic Chapel, Airdrie, Lanarkshire

St Margaret's was the first Roman Catholic church built in Lanarkshire since the Reformation. Its 'flat-Classical' design is distinctive, and was deliberately chosen for this site. It was constructed in 1839.

The steeple of Alexandria Chapel of Ease (Alexandria Old Parish Church), Dunbartonshire

When this church was built in 1840 Alexandria, and the neighbouring communities of Bonhill and Renton, were important centres of calico-printing. The nearest parish church was on the east bank of the River Leven, in Bonhill. This unusual steeple was probably intended to be a landmark. **A**

61

New Marnoch Parish Church (Marnoch Parish Church), Aberchirder, Banffshire

Aberchirder, locally known as 'Foggieloan' is in the historic parish of Marnoch. In 1840 the parishioners of Marnoch violently resisted the imposition of a new minister by the local heritors (landowners). In that context they built this church in the village, in 1840, in a foretaste of the creation of the Free Church at the Disruption in 1843.

Scalloway Parish Church, Shetland

Scalloway is a fishing village on the west coast of the Mainland of Shetland. This very plain parish church was constructed in 1840-41 to serve the community. The porch was probably added in 1871-72.

The West Parish Church (Westburn Parish Church), Greenock, Renfrewshire

The body of this large burgh church was built in 1841 to designs by David Cousin. It was constructed to replace the 16th century Old West Church on the waterfront. The church is in the then-fashionable West End of Greenock facing up Brisbane Street. The tall and elegant steeple was added in 1853.

John Knox Parish Church, Stewarton, Ayrshire

This church was built in 1841-42 for a congregation with a complex denominational history. It was constructed by Rankin and Gemmell of Kilmarnock.

St Mary's Roman Catholic Chapel, Calton, Glasgow

This large church was the second post-Reformation Roman Catholic church to be built in what is now Glasgow. When it was constructed, in 1841-41, the burgh of Calton was independent of Glasgow. This church was intended primarily to accommodate the Irish immigrants who had moved to the area to work in spinning mills and weaving factories. The architect is currently unknown.

The Scottish Episcopal Church of St James, Cruden, Aberdeenshire

A prominent feature in its rural landscape, St James's was designed by William Hay and built in 1842-43, as an early expression of the revival of the Scottish Episcopal Church in north-east Scotland. It is another pioneering example of a steepled Gothic Revival church.